Henna Is . . .

For my sisters: Raazieh, Aliya, Zehra, and my soul
sister, Fatimah. Like henna, your presence infuses
my life with color and celebration! —M. A.

For my family —A. C.

A Feiwel and Friends Book
An imprint of Macmillan Publishing Group, LLC
120 Broadway, New York, NY 10271 · mackids.com

Our books may be purchased in bulk for promotional, educational, or business use. Please contact your local bookseller or the Macmillan
Corporate and Premium Sales Department at (800) 221-7945 ext. 5442 or by email at MacmillanSpecialMarkets@macmillan.com.

Library of Congress Cataloging-in-Publication Data is available.

First edition, 2024
Book design by Mariam Quraishi
Art created with Photoshop CC and Procreate on iPad Pro
Feiwel and Friends logo designed by Filomena Tuosto
Printed in China by RR Donnelley Asia Printing Solutions, Ltd., Dongguan City, Guangdong Province

ISBN 978-1-250-86266-2 (hardcover)
1 3 5 7 9 10 8 6 4 2

Please do not apply henna to pets or other animals.

Henna Is . . .

Written by **Marzieh Abbas**   Illustrated by **Anu Chouhan**

Feiwel and Friends
New York

Henna is nature

Seeds sprouted into shrubs
    leaves kissed by tropical rain
Plucked and dried
    under the golden sun
Pounded to powder
    sieved through mesh

But henna is so much more . . .

Henna is proportion

A squeeze of sour lemon juice
A scoop of sparkling sugar
A splash of oils:
     pine, juniper, cardamom, lavender
Powder becoming paste
Spooned into cones
     like frosting in an icing bag
     ready to decorate

But henna is so much more . . .

Henna is color

The orange of juicy mangoes
    ripe off the tree

Bright and smooth green
    pearly shades of olive and jade

Sun-kissed brown
    deep, dark, and warm

Black like kohl and the
    feathers of crows

But henna is so much more . . .

Henna is texture

Sticky, stretchy paste
    dried to a scratchy crust
    until it all crumbles away
    leaving behind a temporary tattoo

But henna is so
much more . . .

Henna is fragrance
Earthy
Nutty
Lemony
Clove-y

Unique, yet familiar
The fragrance of fields
    mingled with the scent of celebration

But henna is so
    much more . . .

Henna is place

South Asian

North and East African

Middle Eastern

Art connecting eras,

     communities, space, and time

     tradition carried across lands and oceans

But henna is so much more . . .

Henna is technique

Painted patterns
    intricate, interwoven, precise
Seeping beneath a canvas of skin
It tingles and twitches
    as tradition fills every pore
Darkened with steam or roasting cloves,
    the stunning stain lingers for days

But henna is so much more . . .

Henna is art

Flowers and feathers
    scrolls and vines
    geometrical, symmetrical
    a story told through symbols

But henna is so much more . . .

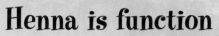

Henna is function

Beautifying

Conditioning

Cooling

Healing

Marking

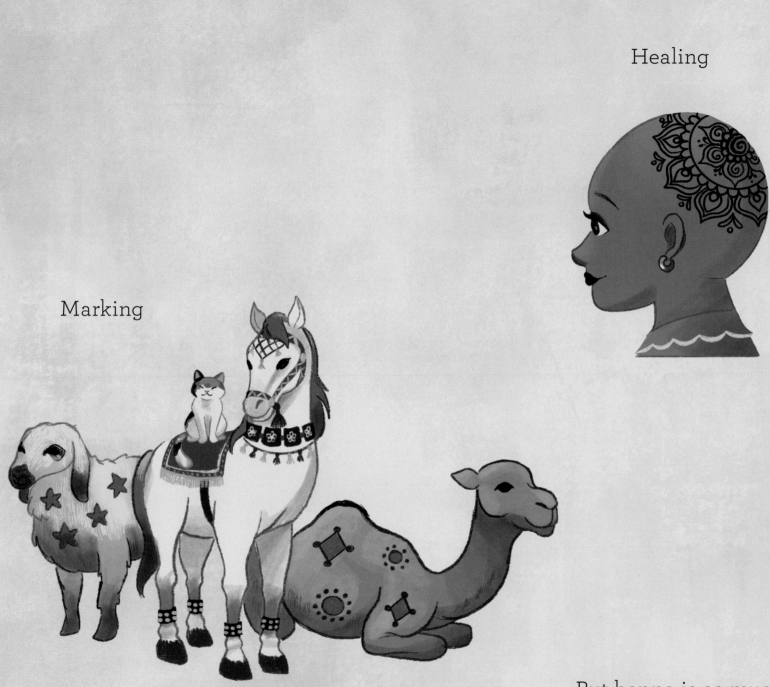

But henna is so much more . . .

Henna is friendship

A guessing game of hidden codes
A challenge just for fun
Wet hennaed palms high-five
    twinning the design
    mirrored like smiles
A friendship sealed

But henna is so much more . . .

Henna is celebration

Eid henna for Muslims
Diwali henna for Hindus
Gracing weddings, birthdays, and baby showers
    joyous gatherings for all

But henna is so much more . . .

Henna is tradition

Making an offering
Bringing prosperity
Keeping bad spirits at bay
Ringing in new beginnings

But henna is so much more than nature, proportion, color, texture, fragrance, place, technique, art, function, friendship, celebration, and tradition . . .

Henna is identity.

Author's Note

Henna is a form of temporary body art that is believed to have originated roughly nine thousand years ago in North Africa and traveled east to India during the Muslim Mughal era. It has since spread all around the world and is now a popular form of temporary tattooing.

Henna artists hide messages in motifs that stain arms, feet, and foreheads. The messages may be symbols—like lotus flowers, peacocks, and butterflies—or names and initials, especially the names of grooms on the hands of their brides.

Other than its decorative purposes, henna also has medicinal healing properties and serves as a conditioner and a natural dye for hair. It is also widely used to mark cattle, thus replacing more intrusive techniques of heat stamping used in the past.